Come Count with Me

Learn to count to Ten in English, Spanish, French and Japanese. Also learn the biblical meaning of each number.

ALOYSIUS M. COLIN

Paperback: 978-1-963050-53-0
eBook: 978-1-963050-54-7
Library of Congress Control Number: 2023923551

Ordering Information:

Prime Seven Media
518 Landmann St.
Tomah City, WI 54660

Printed in the United States of America

Come Count with me: Let's sing along

- **1, 2, 3**
- **Come Count with me.**

- **4, 5, 6**
- **That's our pick**

Continue Song:

- **7, 8, 9**
  - We are doing fine
- **And 10**
  - We're at the end.

Come count with me

1 **English = One**

- **Spanish = Uno**

- **French = Un**

- **Japanese = Ichi (Itchy)**

- **Biblical meaning: Unification, Oneness and Unity.**

Come count with me

- **2 English = Two**
  - **Spanish = Dos**
  - **French = Deux**
  - **Japanese = Ni (knee)**

- **Biblical meaning of Two: Dualism, multiplicity, union, division, and validation.**

Come count with me

- **3** **English = Three**
  - **Spanish = Tres**
  - **French = Trois**
  - **Japanese = San (Sun)**

- **Biblical meaning: Divine wholeness, completeness and perfection.**

Come count with me

- **4** **English = Four**

  - **Spanish = Quatro**

  - **French = Quatre**

  - **Japanese = Shi (She)**

- **Biblical meanings: creation, the world and seasons.**

Come count with me

- **5** **English = Five**
  - **Spanish = Cinco**
  - **French = Cino**
  - **Japanese = Go (Go)**

- **Biblical meaning: God's grace, mercy and favor.**

Come count with me

- **6** **English = Six**
  - **Spanish = Seis**
  - **French = Six (Sis)**
  - **Japanese = Roku (Row Coo)**

- **Biblical meaning: Imperfection, sin, weakness.**

Come Count with me

- **7** **English = Seven**
  - **Spanish = Siete**
  - **French = Sept (Set)**
  - **Japanese = Nana**

- **Biblical meaning: Full and complete**

Come Count with me

- **8** **English = Eight**
  - **Spanish = Ocho**
  - **French = Huit**
  - **Japanese = Hachi**
- **Biblical meaning: New beginnings, a new order or creation.**

Come Count with me

- **9** **English = Nine**
  - **Spanish = Nueve**
  - **French = Neut**
  - **Japanese = Ku (coo)**

- **Biblical meaning: Divine Completeness**

Come Count with me

- **10** **English = Ten**

  - **Spanish = Diez**

  - **French = Dix**

  - **Japanese = Ju (Jew)**

- **Bibblical meaning: Authority, completeness, order, and divine perfection.**

Come count with me.
Sing an old rhyme

Taken from Oxford Dictionary of Nursery Rhymes

- **One, Two buckle my shoe;**

- **Three, Four, knock at the door;**

- **Five ,Six, pick up sticks;**

- **Seven, Eight, lay them straight;**

- **Nine, Ten, a big fat hen**.

Come count with me and sing a new song

- **Sing Along with me:**
- **1, 2, 3**
- **Come count with me**
- **4, 5, 6**
- **That's our pick**
- **7, 8, 9**
- **We are out of time**
- **And 10**
- **We are at the END.**